Introduction

We all know that involving parents in their children's education makes sense. It helps to:

- raise standards of pupil attainment;
- develop children's confidence;
- improve pupil recruitment;
- extend the range of educational opportunities that schools can offer;
- improve the quality of parenting;
- re-engage those parents who have become switched off from learning.

Governments have recently begun to say that they want parents to be more involved in their children's school. The school system should respond better to the needs and aspirations of parents, and every parent should be confident that the system is delivering for their child.

Of course it has not always been like this. For many decades, centuries even, although schools were legally operating under the concept of 'in loco parentis', parents were not welcome at all. The job of educating children wa one for teachers alone.

Gradually, attitudes began to change as society became more open (in the 1960s) and more consumer focused (in the 1990s).

Today there is a range of exciting new opportunities opening up for teachers who want to *really* involve parents.

More primary schools are opening their doors to children of pre-school age. More secondary schools are considering the ways in which they can offer learning opportunities for their community. And the idea of 'full-service schools' – schools that provide a broad range of social services in an effort to redress social disadvantage – is gaining currency.

Of course there are major differences between primary and secondary schools. Involving parents seems a natural thing to do when you are teaching young children. But as soon as those children turn into hormonal teenagers (who are challenging their parents and may not be keen to see them in a school setting) it becomes much more difficult.

In too many schools, there is still a lingering sense that parents are an unwelcome intrusion into an already stressful and overcrowded day. Despite some warm rhetoric (the home/school agreement, for example) there is little real appetite for genuine engagement and partnership.

All the research shows just how critically important parents are to schools. Yet few teachers really take parents seriously. We urgently need a change of mind-set.

But how will this happen in reality? What can schools do to engage parents more effectively and in ways that seem appropriate to parents, teachers and the children they both care for? How can we convince parents that they really are welcome?

These are some of the issues that we will be exploring in this book.

Understanding parents' needs

Lack of confidence

Ever noticed the way that some parents hover outside, apparently not feeling confident enough to come in? Or wondered why otherwise mild-looking parents seem to be unduly aggressive when talking to you about their child?

They probably lack confidence. Perhaps their own experiences of school were not happy ones. Or perhaps they are currently suffering from low self-esteem because a relationship has gone wrong. Maybe they simply find schools intimidating.

It may well be that your school is unnecessarily bureaucratic or unfriendly to parents. A simple way of finding this out is to try the 'parent experience' for yourself. With the agreement of school staff, think of all the different reasons why a parent might want to contact a teacher. Then 'walk' them through to help you see what it might be like. Call the main switchboard and see how it feels. 'Arrive' at school on spec to see a teacher and see what happens to you.

While the role of a teacher is not to be a social worker for pupil's parents, common sense suggests that putting all parents at their ease is going to be helpful.

Why is it that so many schools inadvertently put off the very people whose help they really need – parents? Make a serious attempt to speak in everyday English, get better at planning ahead and try to understand your pupils' home lives, and you can really make a difference.

Application

Try these simple ideas to put parents at their ease:

- Offer to visit every parent in their home before their child comes to school.

- Ask parents how they like to be communicated with (phone, letter, email) and in what language.

- Have a barbeque or picnic at the end of the summer holidays so that parents can meet other parents.

- Have named photos of all staff – teachers and support staff – in the foyer, along with a drawing of each member of staff by children.

- Put the name of each teacher and teaching assistant on doors of classrooms.

- Send a personally signed 'how to contact me' letter to all new parents.

- Use simple, non-jargonistic words.

- Send friendly notes every Wednesday during the first term.

- Have comfortable adult-sized chairs in the classrooms, in corridors and in the foyer.

- Don't sit at your desk when parents meet you in your classroom.

- Have a water machine in the foyer.

- Offer parents a free coffee or tea every second Monday after they have dropped off their child.

- Each year ask parents what you could do to make the school more welcoming.

Technique

Educational jargon and gobbledegook

Why do so many schools write letters that seem to assume that their parents are professors of education? Why do teachers sometimes blind parents with gobbledegook?

The answer to both of these questions is simple. Teachers become familiar with their own professional vocabulary and stop noticing it. We talk about vertical grouping as if it is clear that this is about different year groups being taught in the same class, as opposed to something in the school's diet that encourages very tall children. And many UK schools still call their pre-term and term-time training days INSET (sometimes called insect days by children!). Some even still refer to their moments of 'freedom' as Baker days in continuing homage to a man that many used to hate!

The key to being jargon free is to maintain a healthy sense of humour and spot all the strange words and phrases that creep into the daily vocabulary of a teacher!

Application

Play educational baloney bingo. Use this simple bingo card whenever a colleague is writing or talking to parents:

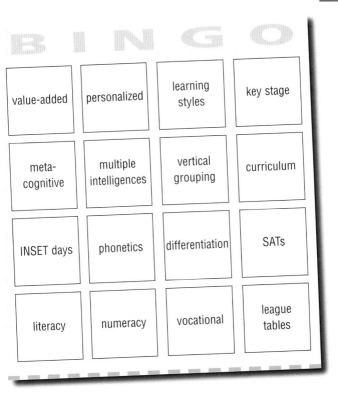

value-added	personalized	learning styles	key stage
meta-cognitive	multiple intelligences	vertical grouping	curriculum
INSET days	phonetics	differentiation	SATs
literacy	numeracy	vocational	league tables

Now make up your own bingo card, and using it to help you, go through every single document you send to parents and remove or explain each of these words.

You might like to have a parent group dedicated to being your jargon spotters and giving you feedback if any educational baloney creeps through.

Technique

Advance planning

Ever felt irritated that the parents you really wanted to see did not turn up for a parents evening? Or wondered why a few pupils always seem to turn up when you have closed the school for a training day? Or perhaps, as a secondary-school teacher, you have despaired about the late arrival of coursework or homework?

There may be good reasons for all of these; it may simply be pupil error, forgetfulness or downright cussedness! But often it is attributable to a school's own advance planning system. Look at most local authority websites and you can find out the dates of school terms for the next three or more years. Yet when parents ask which days will be training days in the next term, they are often met with blank looks. To parents, such looks speak volumes. They imply that the business of running a school is far more important than the job of parenting, and that the school will tell you when it is ready.

Of course, schools also need to be able to be spontaneous and offer activities or trips that do not appear on forward plans. You can always flag these up on your website, or by using reminder posters at all the entrances to the school.

But this is not an excuse for just-in-time planning!

See p19 and p32 for other related ideas.

Application

ell before each school year

- Check term dates for the year ahead.

- Agree school closure dates.

- Check on any local authority or network or cluster activities.

- Add in all major public holidays and festivals.

- Decide on dates of all major school events.

- Decide on dates of all major assessment and curriculum activities.

the start of each term

blish a detailed calendar of the term:

- online;

- in large format (and possibly in other languages) to go up in the foyer;

- on paper for parents;

- on paper for pupils.

the end of each week

nd pupils home with a 'Things to remember for next week' sheet.

the end of each day

nd pupils home with a 'Things to remember for tomorrow' sheet.

Technique

Complex families

What do you know about the families of the children who come to your school? How many children that you teach:

- live with one parent?

- have stepbrothers or stepsisters?

- have a step-parent?

- spend some weekends in another home?

- spend some nights during the week at another home?

- have a parent who works in the evening or at night?

- have a parent whose job requires them to move home every few years?

- speak more than one language?

- have a parent who can barely understand or speak English?

- travel for more than 40 minutes to get to school each day?

- arrived in the country in the last few months?

- are going through difficult family times?

More and more children go home to 'blended' families where one parent may not be a biological parent, or where there are other children or other adults living under the same roof.

While teachers may feel that many aspects of a child's home life are necessarily 'off limits', the more empathy an understanding of different kinds of family circumstances, the more likely it is that all parents will be really involved.

Application

a parent works as a nurse and is often on night shifts, then it may be very difficult for him or her ever to come to typical parent's evening. Family circumstances are likely to affect availability, communication, supervision and confidence.

Look at each of the examples here and imagine:

- ■ what impact it might have
- ■ what your school could do to help.

Circumstance	Impact	How to help
One parent		
Recent immigrant		
Family moves home regularly		
Long journey to school		
Lots of step siblings		
Two homes		

Technique

Frequently asked questions

Ever stopped to wonder why you often get asked the same question by parents? Or realized that newly qualified teachers do not know many of the answers? Have you ever felt concerned that questions concerning national education policy may get answered in different ways by your staff? Or just felt that it was downright inefficient to keep 'reinventing the wheel'?

Then you need to gather together all the frequently asked questions with their 'approved' answers.

Here are a few to get you going. But you may like to come up with you own list, plus the right answers to each question.

- Where can I find out about local schools and nurseries?
- How do I get a secondary place for my child?
- How do I find out about school term dates?
- Can my child go home during the day?
- Can my child cycle to school?
- Can my child go on holiday during term-time?
- Is there anywhere my child can leave things safely at school?
- What do I do if my child is sick?
- How do I get extra help for my child?
- What do I do if I think my child is being bullied?
- How do I know if the school is closed for bad weather?
- How much homework should my child get?
- How can I get involved?
- Can I get help to improve my English?
- How much TV should my child watch?

Application

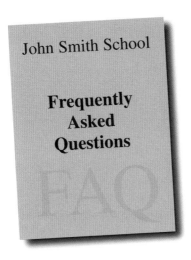

John Smith School

Frequently Asked Questions

FAQ

Make a guide for parents with frequently asked questions (FAQs). To help you get started:

✓ Think of every aspect of school life.

✓ Now imagine you are a parent; what might you want to know?

✓ Next, brainstorm all the questions you have ever been asked by parents.

1 Ask each member of staff to come up with ten questions.

2 Finally, pool them all and sort them into the ones most likely to be asked.

Getting better at communicating

Technique

The front desk

You are an anxious parent who has come to school on a matter of great importance. The first person you see is the caretaker, who is friendly but vague. Then you get to something that looks like the reception area, but there is a pane of glass between you and the receptionist, who is surrounded by mounds of paper, talking on the phone and looking everywhere except in your direction.

Or maybe it's like this. You are an anxious parent who has come to school on a matter of great importance. You get to the reception area and are greeted efficiently but with no warmth, no empathy and by someone who is really too busy to stop and spend time with you.

Recognize either of them? Of course it never happens like this in schools, does it?!

The person who looks after the front desk is, in many ways, the most important person in the whole school when it comes to communicating with parents. It may be a receptionist, a secretary, a volunteer or a teacher – or perhaps it's the headteacher…

The welcome function is so important that there are two parts of this guide dealing with it. You can read more about the reception experience on p34 and p35.

Think of all the ways you use communication in your private and professional life. Now apply all of these to the way you communicate with parents. Technology can help you personalize contact and allow you to manage the demands on your time, while giving a much better service to parents.

Application

What kind of school do you work in? What first impression do you want to create? It helps to know, so you can make sure that the first point of communication for many parents puts this into practice.

Look at these words. Add some of your own to the list. Then choose the five that most sum up the impression you want to create for parents.

welcoming

academic

caring

supportive

successful

flexible

child-friendly

business-friendly

adult-friendly

about learning

about achieving potential

radical

different

Technique

Letters and emails

Ever had a letter that starts 'Dear Bill Lucas'? Or that is not signed by the person who sent it? Or that is a personal letter home about your child beginning 'Dear Parent'? Or has the wrong phone number on it? Or that is sent out on 5 April with a date that just says 'March' on it?

If you are a parent, I bet you have! Maybe you've written them, too! There is only one thing worse than that sort of letter, and that's an appointment letter from your hospital written in a confusing mix of upper and lower-case letters and often mail-merged in such a way that your name is back to front in the name field…

Talking of which, why do schools not mail-merge letters to parents so that they can use the name and form of greeting that parents have said they prefer, rather than opting for the lazy 'Dear Parent'?

And why doesn't every school keep an email address for each parent who has one, and automatically send an email version of every hard-copy letter to it? It's bizarre that schools use email so rarely. Of course it takes time, but so do telephone calls, letters and meetings!

In fact, why do we still use pupils as messenger pigeons?! In the information age, why not actively seek to bypass pupils and talk direct to parents?

Application

Have a staff discussion about how email could help you involve more parents more effectively.

Just wanted you to know that Amanda has done a beautiful painting in art today; you might like to chat to her about it.
A. Teacher

I emailed you at ten, 12 and a few minutes ago and you have not replied yet; what's going on?
A. Parent

Can you pop in tomorrow morning when you drop Toby off to pick up some books?
A. Teacher

Technique

Newsletters and e-zines

Why are too many school newsletters a disappointment? Is it because busy teachers leave it to the last moment, maybe even the day before the end of term, so that the news somehow seems irrelevant?

The best newsletters are a joy to read. There are no boundaries – except your imagination – as to what they can include. The simplest way to get your creative juices flowing is to look at 20 or so examples from other schools and shamelessly borrow other people's good ideas! And with email and good design programs, your parents can read it in full colour if they want to!

Here are a few suggestions:

- Keep it short and regular.
- Use a simple computer program so that the format is easy to create.
- Make sure each class or year gets a different version or a special supplement so that parents always know

    a) what is going to be taught in the next month;

    b) how it will be taught;

    c) what they can do to help.

- Include pupils' work.
- Use lots of photographs.
- Get parents to contribute.
- Talk about forthcoming events.

TIP:
If your school ever finds itself in difficult times or there is a terrible local or national event, consider sending a brief newsletter home every day.

Application

Use the prompts on this page to get you thinking about how you can make your school's newsletter regular, dynamic and read!

events

invitations

REMINDERS

thank-yous

explanations

how-tos

photos

pupils' work

cartoons

trips

Technique

Notice boards and displays

Some people say that they can evaluate a school within minutes of being in the reception area, just from the way the environment is organized – especially the notice boards and displays. Wooden cases full of silver cups give out one kind of message, for example, while eye-catching displays of children's work give out another.

It is easy to assume that notice boards and displays are simply a mixture of important information for visitors to school, along with a few examples of children's work.

In the technological age, you do not need just to confine yourself to this kind of display. Many schools have a large TV screen on show, displaying still photos, film, pages from the school's website or even their own daily TV broadcasts.

Or it could be that you choose to make creative use of three-dimensional artefacts, designed by pupils, staff, alumni of the school or by sculptors.

> **TIP:**
> Designate a special area in school that is specifically for parents to communicate with other parents.

Application

What do you already have on display in your school (or in any other school that you know)? What do you like and what could be improved?

Which of these do you have?

- Pictures of inspirational role models
- Motivational sayings
- Famous quotations
- Learning tips
- Curious questions
- TV screens with live information
- Sculpture
- Puzzles
- Displays of children's work in progress
- Trophies
- Award certificates
- Photographs of school people.

Give your school's display a makeover. It might be a good opportunity not just to use a teacher, but also a teaching assistant and a parent to help you.

Telephone contact

Why are some teachers reluctant to use the telephone? Perhaps because, given their busy days, it is so difficult to find time to make calls?

Yet telephone calls are the next best thing to being there. They are a really good way of maintaining communication with parents. And in this age of voicemail and texting, it's easier than ever to reach parents by phone.

> **TIP:**
> Set aside times each day when you can receive (and make) calls and let parents know of these.

y some of these ideas:

- Make a point of calling at least one parent a week to share some good news about their child – a 'sunshine call'. Make sure each family receives at least two of these during the school year.

- Create a database of contact information – correct surname, home, work and mobile numbers and preferred time of calls.

- Keep track of any call you make, whether good news or bad. Make a note of the date, nature of the call, parents' responses and outcomes.

- Make your first call to any parent a positive one. One good idea is to make welcoming calls just before the new school year begins.

- Prioritize those parents who don't respond to written invitations to parents' evenings. A call lets them know you're interested.

Technique

Homework diaries

At secondary school, homework diaries (or similar) are an essential means of communicating between home and school. Although increasingly disregarded by pupils as the become older, they offer a parent the chance:

- to verify their offspring's claim that they do not have any homework to do;
- to scribble a quick comment or question to the form tutor.

At primary level, they are used less, mainly because of understandable uncertainty about the role of homework in the early years. However, many primary schools see the benefit of using some kind of diary.

Whatever phase of education your school is in, there are some essential questions to answer:

- What is your homework policy?
- What kinds of work do you encourage?
- How do you ensure that it's spread evenly for pupils?
- What do you want parents to do?
  - Check that it's being set?
  - Help their child / not help their child?
  - Write comments?

TIP:
To make sure that your homework diary is the best it can be, look at 20 examples from different schools and choose the best of them!

Application

Diary

ook at these different approaches. What do you want
our school to include in your homework diaries?

Top tips for parents

How to be a better learner

What kind of a learner are you?

How to plan your week

Where to do homework

Term-time diary

Useful websites

Technique

Reports

Ever written reports that are a masterpiece of blandness because you can't quite remember the pupil? Or wondered what the impact of receiving a report that gives E for attainment and A for effort might be on a pupil with low self-esteem? Or stopped to think whether the reports your school sends parents are at all helpful?

In the UK, schools are obliged to send parents at least one report per year on each child (in addition to the annual report about the school as a whole). These need to include:

- Brief comments on a pupil's progress in each subject and activity studied as part of the school curriculum, highlighting strengths and development needs.

- A description of the pupil's general progress.

- Arrangements for parents to discuss the report with a teacher at the school.

- A summary of the pupil's attendance record during the period to which the information in the report relates.

At the end of Key Stages 3 and 4, there are additional requirements for schools to provide information on pupils' attainment levels (SATs and GCSEs).

But apart from these relatively vague requirements, headteachers are free to do what they want.

Application

Use this activity to reflect on the effectiveness of your own school's reports.

Report on the effectiveness of your school's reports

Name of school: _____

Effort	How hard are you trying? How many other school reports have you analysed? Have you asked parents what they think? How are pupils involved? How often do you produce reports and why?
Attainment	How useful are your school reports? Have you asked parents? Have you compared them with reports from other schools? What research evidence have you considered in helping you to decide what information to include? How much guidance and training have staff received?

Technique

Assessment for Learning

Reports about assessment in schools are consistently critical. Marking is frequently inconsistent, and reports to parents often fail to describe the strengths and weaknesses of pupils and retreat into bland 'could do better' statements.

Yet the research into what is now known as Assessment for Learning has shown that it need not be like this. Assessment for Learning is the process of seeking and interpreting evidence for use by learners and their teachers to decide where the learners are in their learning, where they need to go and how best to get there.

It is essentially about learners giving and receiving feedback that can be used by them to improve the way they learn.

Application

Using the ten principles of Assessment for Learning (A4L) listed below, ask yourself how you could involve parents in the assessment process more effectively. For example, how do you deal with the emotional impact of the assessment in the reports you send parents? How do you share assessment criteria with parents?

1. A4L should be part of effective planning of teaching and learning.

2. A4L should focus on how pupils learn.

3. A4L should be recognized as central to classroom practice.

4. A4L should be regarded as a key professional skill for teachers.

5. A4L should be sensitive and constructive because any assessment has an emotional impact.

6. Assessment should take account of learner motivation.

7. A4L should promote commitment to learning goals and a shared understanding of the criteria by which they are assessed.

8. Learners should receive constructive guidance about how to improve.

9. A4L develops learners' capacity for self-assessment so that they can become reflective and self-monitoring.

10. A4L should recognize the full range of achievements of all learners.

Technique

Websites

Not so long ago, very few schools had websites. Now every school has one.

Some are little more than a set of documents with a few photographs. Others allow a parent to email their child's teacher directly, book appointments online and shop for school uniforms in a virtual environment – all the while being sponsored by local businesses.

So, why do you have a website?

No, I mean what is the real reason? Some possible answers include:

- Because other schools have one.
- For parents to visit.
- For children to visit.
- To show children's work.
- To make your school look good.

What about you?

Which are the websites that your staff and your parents like and use most? Amazon? eBay? What features do commercial sites use that might be of use to yours? And what about educational sites?

Application

Use these questions to review your current website.

1. What does it say about your school? What do you want it to say?

2. What 'feel' do you want it to have? Informative? Fun? Interactive? Friendly?

3. Why do you think parents will visit the website? Choosing a school? Talking to a teacher? Finding out things? For their own learning?

4. How easy is it to navigate around?

5. Do you have a link to your home page on every page?

6. How often do you change the information on your site?

7. How many of these do you have?

   ✓ A map of how to get to your school.

   ✓ A map of your school.

   ✓ Photographs of the inside and outside.

   ✓ Photographs of staff and descriptions of what they do.

   ✓ Information for parents, with a prospectus and admission details.

   ✓ A library with all your policy documents.

   ✓ A section for pupils.

   ✓ Links to other educational websites for children and parents.

   ✓ An online shop for books and uniform.

   ✓ Examples of pupils' work.

   ✓ An events diary.

   ✓ Clear contact details.

Remember: **Keep it as simple as possible!**

Technique

Signage and physical space

Why do so many schools have signs like this?

All visitors must report to the school office

Or worse still this:

Danger of death

Of course schools have to be safe places. But they also have to be welcoming, too. It is a simple matter to replace the first sign with:

Welcome to St Bede's School

Please come straight to the office and introduce yourself

And dangerous electricity boxes can be hidden away from public view.

In many primary schools, parents gather at the school gates to pick up their children. Often they wait on a pavement by a road, getting cold and wet if the weather is unkind. It is an ideal moment to share information with them and listen to their views. Why not create a waiting area just inside your school's grounds, with trees, shelter, seats and notice boards?

How can you make parents feel that they are truly welcome in your school? From changes to the physical environment to the imagination with which you make teaching methods accessible, here are some ideas to help you bring the home/school agreement alive.

Application

Which of these signs would you like to see in your school?

Technique

The reception experience

Think of the best hotel you have ever been to. Let the image form in your head. Next, think of the most friendly doctor's waiting room. Then the best airport lounge. Then the best children's shoe shop. Finally, let your mind go wild and try to imagine what would make a nervous parent feel relaxed if they were visiting your reception area for the first time.

Now go and look at your own reception area. How does it compare to the pictures you have been conjuring up? What simple things could you do to improve your reception area? What radical things could you do?

As important as the physical environment is, it is the initial contact with people that matters most. Who is the first person that visitors meet in your school? It is essential that he or she is welcoming, friendly and able to speak normal (as opposed to educational) English. Most importantly, he or she should be clear that dealing with visitors must often take precedence over office work.

Application

Most high-street shops use mystery shoppers, who act as ordinary customers, buy goods and provide a written report about the experience. Why not adapt this idea for your school? It may be sensible to explain to staff what you are going to do, and you will need to persuade half a dozen or so people to act as your mystery parents. You can then share their thoughts, learn from them and improve the reception experience.

Excuse me, I'd like a good education for my children, please. Can you help?

Parent/teacher meetings

Why do parent/teacher meetings so often take place in classrooms, with parents sitting on child-sized seats while the teacher sits behind his or her desk? Why do these meetings often start as much as half an hour late? It's odd that good teachers, who regularly plan and teach excellent lessons, can be so apparently under-prepared for dealing with parents. Perhaps they need a little in-service training.

It all starts with a welcoming and informing teacher mind-set. If you really value parent input, you could publicize all parent/teacher meetings, send personalized invitations, phone parents if you do not hear from them, make it possible to book appointments online and co-ordinate parent visits with visits they make for other siblings in your school.

You might also like to think about flexible timings for meetings. You could offer early-morning or evening meetings, as well as the occasional Saturday morning and escorted home visits for a few.

Try to make clear what are the goals for a meeting, just as you would for the learning outcomes of a lesson.

> **TIP:**
> When a parent arrives for a meeting, stand up to welcome them, and escort them to the door at the end.

Ideally you will make meetings a regular feature of school life, by holding a parent surgery every fortnight and clear publicizing the drop-in times. You might also like to have Parents' Room, if space allows.

Application

Use this checklist to help you plan a good parent/teacher meeting.

Have you:

- [ ] publicized the dates of all parent/teacher meetings at least three times?

- [ ] made sure that the environment is adult and welcoming?

- [ ] provided food and drink?

- [ ] provided a crèche?

- [ ] invited parents personally?

- [ ] remembered to invite both parents of children whose parents have divorced or separated?

- [ ] considered second language needs?

- [ ] decided what is the goal of the meeting?

- [ ] laid out individual pupils' work so that it can be seen easily?

- [ ] decided how you will follow up the meeting?

- [ ] worked out how you can use teaching assistants to support you in the process?

- [ ] attended any training days recently?

- [ ] got any useful tips you can share with colleagues?

Technique

Demonstration lessons

In the opinion of management guru Charles Handy, the privacy of the classroom could be a dangerous thing. This is no longer the case. Teaching assistants, other teaching staff, visiting school inspectors and many other people are likely to drop in to watch you teach!

However, parents very rarely get a glimpse of what actually goes on inside the classroom. They often feel that education has changed so much since they went to school that they would not understand what was going on. The simplest way of overcoming this is to run a series of demonstration lessons for parents throughout the course of each year.

Many teachers still lack confidence about acting out their teacher role in front of parents. This is understandable, because teachers have to develop a style and manner for dealing with children that may feel embarrassing in front of other adults. The simplest way of overcoming such fears is to insist that all teachers teach demonstration lessons (with appropriate support), so that it becomes entirely normal.

Application

The process of planning a demonstration lesson for parents is no different from what you do when you plan a lesson for pupils.

1. Be clear about your objective

What do you want the parents to have learned? An example might be: To have experienced the way we teach reading and begun to understand what they can do to support us.

2. Sell the idea

How will you get parents to attend? You could send out personal invitations, get a few parents to act as your persuaders or use the power of pupil persuasion.

3. Be welcoming

Whereas you may have to tell children to be quiet, you may find it difficult to get adults to talk in class! Work out how you can be as welcoming as possible to allay anyone's nerves. Stress that the emphasis will be on having fun.

4. Be practical

Try to avoid lots of talk. Instead, get parents working on a practical task and then explain what it shows about the way you teach. Or better still, see if they can come up with the answers or ideas.

5. Make it normal.

Offer lots of chances to see demonstration lessons. This will, paradoxically, take the heat off you!

Technique

Family days

In the USA, the national PTA has started a Take Your Family to School Week. The UK's Campaign for Learning also encourages parents to get involved in their children's school during Family Learning Week each year.

But if a week seems a long time, why not start with a single day? While some schools run a family day at the weekend, typically during the summer term when the weather is better, why not be bolder and choose a normal weekday so that parents can really see what school life is like?

Of course, if you open your doors to parents (and grandparents, potentially) it will not, strictly speaking, be a normal day! Think of it as a 'life in the day' of your school.

Even a day like this requires considerable planning, and the involvement and support of many different people. Start preparing for it well in advance. You might like to contact schools that have already done it and get their advice.

Application

se these ideas to get you thinking about what you might
o on your family day:

- Breakfast for parents and children.

- Lunch served by children for parents.

- Cook a meal.

- Maths games in the playground.

- Shared reading sessions.

- Education jargon quiz.

- Learning styles questionnaire.

- Pupil guided tours.

- A trail in the school's grounds.

- A music event.

- Pupil and parent art class and a display.

- Display of photos of parents when they were at school.

- Demonstration lessons.

- Visits from poets, artists, scientists.

- A PTA stall.

- Stalls from local educational attractions.

Technique

The home/school agreement

In the UK, all schools are required by law to have a home/school agreement. The law says:

- All maintained schools, city technology colleges and city colleges for the technology of the arts adopt a home/school agreement and associated parental declaration.

- A home/school agreement is a statement explaining: the school's aims and values; the school's responsibilities towards its pupils who are of compulsory school age; the responsibilities of the pupil's parents; and what the school expects of its pupils.

- Before adopting or revising the home/school agreement, the governing body must consult all registered parents of pupils at the school who are of compulsory school age.

- The governing body must take reasonable steps to ensure that all registered parents of pupils of compulsory school age sign the parental declaration to indicate that they understand and accept the contents of the agreement.

(from The School Standards and Framework Act 1998)

The UK's Department for Education and Skills (DfES) asks governors to consider these points:

- Have you asked parents what they expect from the school?

- What do you expect from parents?

- Have you asked parents what they think of the school?

- How do you involve parents?

- Why do some parents not get involved?

Technique

- What can you do to establish an effective working relationship with the 'missing' parents?

- What can you do to help parents to help their child?

- What priority do teachers give to working with parents?

- What does your school do to listen to the views of pupils?

(from Home-School Agreements, Guidance for Schools)

The DfES also gives guidance on the process of creating a home/school agreement, suggesting the following stages:

1. Discuss with governing body or chair of governors.
2. Discuss with staff, non-teaching staff and partner agencies.
3. Consult parents and carers.
4. Consult with families where English is an additional language.
5. Consult pupils.
6. Draft an agreement.
7. Consult all parents and carers on the draft agreement.
8. Consult pupils on the draft agreement.
9. Redraft the agreement.
10. Seek final approval from governors.
11. Arrange for parents to sign the agreement.
12. Launch the agreement with pupils.

(from www.standards.dfes.gov.uk/parentalinvolvement/hsa/hsa_how)

But while some schools may have followed this kind of process when first introducing a home/school agreement, few do now. Instead, for most schools, the annual signing of the home/school agreement is a rather lacklustre affair, complying with the letter of the law but not its spirit.

Primary v secondary

In the UK, the *Every Child Matters* legislation has introduced other dimensions that schools may wish to consider. It states that pupils should have the support they need to:

- be healthy
- stay safe
- enjoy and achieve
- make a positive contribution
- achieve economic wellbeing.

The nature of parental involvement is different depending on the age of the pupils. At the primary stage, it is important to encourage parents to undertake some of the basic learning support mechanisms, such as reading to their child every day. Later on, it may be more helpful to focus on the parent's role in promoting a healthy lifestyle, for example.

children become young adults, there are other social
essures on parents too!

I thought
I told you to dress
appropriately, Dad!

- Think of five new ways in which your school could involve parents.

- Set up a meeting with parents to discuss how they could be more involved.

Technique

Different kinds of parental involvement

There are four broadly different types of involvement that you may want to encourage, and which might underpin thinking about your agreement. Some inevitably take teachers into sensitive areas of individual lifestyle choices:

1. **Family learning**
   - Providing a home environment that helps children to develop.
   - Finding out how to help their child become an effective learner.

2. **Effective parenting**
   - Ensuring that children have enough sleep and nutritious food.
   - Creating an emotional context in which children can become self-confident.

3. **Supporting school staff**
   - Engaging with teachers by attending meetings and reinforcing messages.
   - Reinforcing school rules on uniform.
   - Coming to school events.

4. **Volunteering**
   - Contributing to the life of the school in some way, for example, by being an extra adult on a school outing
   - Undertaking a formal role such becoming a member of the PTA.

When you are reviewing the effectiveness of your current agreement, you may like to consider all the above issues in order to decide what your approach will be. Opposite are some specific suggestions for the kinds of statement you could include.

> **TIP:**
> Above all, every school needs to have a clear, published plan for involving parents more in school...have you got one?

Application

Many home/school agreements include a set of statements. Use these to discuss what yours might include if you choose to update it.

Parents agree to:

- ensure my child attends school properly;
- see that my child arrives at school promptly;
- make sure I/we notify school of any absence;
- support school's guidelines on behaviour;
- support my child with homework;
- create opportunities for learning at home;
- ensure my child goes to bed at a reasonable time on weekdays;
- attend parent meetings;
- reply to letters from school;
- talk to the school if I am worried about my child.

Pupils/students agree to:

- always try to do my best in lessons;
- remember to be polite and thoughtful to others;
- always try to enjoy school and help others to do the same;
- talk at home about what I learn at school;
- do all the homework I am set;
- be on time;
- talk to my teacher if I am unhappy about something;
- try to exercise my learning 'muscles'.

Providing practical support

Technique

Clubs

In the last few years there has been considerable interest in breakfast, homework and after-school clubs. At the same time, many schools have found it increasingly difficult to provide more traditional lunchtime and after-school clubs, due to the many other demands on teachers.

A breakfast club is a place where children can be dropped off before school and enjoy breakfast together. It might be run by school staff or qualified play workers. Astonishingly, one in five children leaves home without any kind of breakfast. Schools that run these clubs report better attendance, concentration and wellbeing as a consequence. The charity ContinYou (www.continyou.org.uk) has developed many resources to help schools set up breakfast clubs.

An after-school club is a place for children to go after the school day has finished, usually from around 3.30pm to 6pm. It is normally staffed by qualified play workers, who lay on a range of games, sports and crafts activities. Sometimes play workers will escort children from the school to the club. A homework club, as its name suggests, normally provides some kind of one-to-one support for children who cannot go home or who choose to get extra help.

There are many practical ways in which you can support parents. Dip into these suggestions and try something new.

4

Application

Follow these steps to set up your own breakfast club.

Stage 1: Decide what kind of club you want

- Cereal, toast and juice – easy to do without involving catering staff.
- Servery/canteen – more like a school lunch using catering staff.
- Community kitchen – run by the community and could open to families, too.

Stage 2: Plan it

- Who is it for?
- Who will run it?
- How will you fund it? (Local authorities can sometimes help.)
- Where will it be?
- When will it happen?
- How will you market it?

Stage 3: Get support

You might like to marshal all the evidence for the benefits of breakfast clubs before talking to as many of your parents and pupils as possible.

Stage 4: Start a club

Good Luck!

Technique

Parent workshops

In the last few years, schools have begun to realize that, as well as teaching children, they can help parents continue their development as lifelong learners. If you can engage parents and help them to engage with their children's education, then you are likely to improve the performance of pupils in your school. You are also likely to find the parents really beginning to understand more about what you are doing!

Of course, adults learn in different ways from children. They come with lots of personal experiences, many of them negative. They can have strong views about education and parenting. They have other responsibilities and other priorities; any workshop you run will have to compete with these. And they are much more likely to want to know how they can use what they are learning.

Application

When you are running a session for parents you need to be much more like a facilitator than a teacher. Consider these ten dos and don'ts:

1. Always use people's names.

2. Remember that we all learn in different ways.

3. Encourage involvement by minimizing the anxious moments.

4. Make it safe to take part.

5. Avoid too much 'teacher talk'.

6. Be aware of the importance of open and supportive communication, including your body language.

7. Take care over the way you choose words.

8. Avoid giving unhelpful labels or making premature assumptions.

9. Be sensitive when you put people into groups.

10. Be careful whenever you choose a case study or example; it may wrongly be assumed to be the 'best' or 'only' way.

Helping parents to become learning coaches

What do you say when parents ask what they can do to help their child? Perhaps you talk about homework, or something specific like reading. While both these kinds of activities may be useful, you might also consider helping parents to become effective learning coaches.

Coaching involves helping a child to find out how he or she is doing and what he or she can do to improve. Every parent can learn to become a coach, giving their child feedback as a natural part of daily life. Coaching always involves accentuating the positive. Parents can also learn how to focus on one issue at a time, rather than making general sweeping statements. It's important to focus on what a child is doing, rather than criticize his or her personality.

Timing is important, too. The closer to an event that you can give feedback, the better. But if a child is very distressed, it may be more helpful to calm him or her down first.

TIP:
You might like to try the RESPECT method yourself (see opposite). Then use it in a parent workshop. Get parents to practise it in pairs, either with their own partner or with another parent so that they can start to feel comfortable with using positive comments.

Application

The words which go to make up RESPECT suggest seven different ways of giving advice and feedback to a child (or adult).

Reassuring	'I know you thought this would be a good way of doing this and…'
Enthusiastic	'I really liked the way you…'
Steady	'That's okay. I'll wait until you pick them all up again…'
Practical	'Let's see what happens when we try this again. You stand over there and I'll…'
Engaging	'I'll do it first and then you try…'
Clear	'When you move your hand more slowly, you will stop smudging your writing…'
Truthful	'You're not as good at kicking with your left foot as you are with your right…'

(from *Help your Child to Succeed*, Network Educational Press)

Practise these kinds of approaches by imagining specific situations in which to try it out. If you want to have some fun, see if you can coach a person to throw a tennis ball over their shoulder into a bucket that you have put three paces behind them!

This exercise helps to reassure you (and parents) that you can be an effective coach without having to be an expert.

Helping parents create learning homes

Do you ever worry that it does not matter what you do at school because it is all going to be 'undone' as soon as the child goes home? Maybe you have a picture of a home in which the television is on until late at night in a child's bedroom, for example?

Most teachers would like to offer advice to parents, but would be unwilling to come across as judgemental. A good way in to this subject is by talking about it in more general terms at a parent workshop. You could start by asking parents to remember what their own homes were like when they were growing up. Then encourage them to talk about what they do now.

Every room has the potential for good educational activities and parents are their children's first and most powerful teachers. In the kitchen, cooking can involve maths and the use of instructions. Eating together is a good time for family members to talk together and plan ahead. You can make it fun by playing word games. Even the bathroom provides opportunities for basic science!

Issues you may want to debate are the amount of TV, the use of computers and the internet, bedtimes and how to encourage reading. By posing questions, you can avoid appearing to be the heavy hand of school and position yourself as the parent's friend. The more you can show that all parents (including teachers) have to wrestle with tough issues about the use of the home, the better.

Application

ncourage parents to survey their homes and see how they
an get the best out of the space they have. Talk through
ow this might be done using these simple instructions.

(From *Help Your Child to Succeed*, Network Continuum Press)

1. Create a floor plan of home.

2. Have a family discussion about the things you do or could
   do in each room that might help a child's education.

3. Write the activities on sticky notes and stick them to the
   appropriate rooms. For example:

   ■ Learning to cook in the kitchen.
   ■ Using a computer in the living room.
   ■ Learning about plants in the garden.
   ■ Learning about where food comes from by looking at
     tins and packets.

courage parents to come up with their own rules on
ings like the amount of TV their children watch and the
e of the computer. You might like to discourage parents
om allowing their children to have TVs or computers (if
ey have internet access) in their bedrooms.

Technique

Helping parents discover classrooms on their doorsteps

Ask yourself if you know where to find your nearest:

- ☐ Library
- ☐ Museum
- ☐ Historic house
- ☐ Farm
- ☐ Animal sanctuary
- ☐ Art gallery
- ☐ Theatre
- ☐ Cinema
- ☐ Leisure centre
- ☐ College
- ☐ Sports club
- ☐ Scouts/Guides group
- ☐ Internet café.

If not, why not? Most learning is informal. It results from an interest. Many schools have lots of useful resources on their doorsteps, yet surprisingly few actively promote them to parents.

Why doesn't every school have a large wall map showing where all the local educational attractions are and providing a big rack of leaflets about them for parents?

TIP:
Establish special relationships with your local attractions, possibly including price reductions if relevant.

Application

ave a look at a large-scale map of your area. How far
ight most parents be prepared to travel to visit places on
ot, by bus, by train or by car?

ark a realistic area on the map. Then systematically find
ut what educational resources there are within that area
nd produce a 'classrooms on your doorstep' map for your
ception area.

(From *Help Your Child to Succeed*, Network Continuum Press)

Technique

Behaviour management

It is very easy for parents to blame teachers and teachers t
blame parents when a child's behaviour breaks down.
Parents and teachers, being individuals, are bound to have
different views of what kind of behaviour is acceptable.

But in reality, parents and teachers are natural allies. Each
needs the other, and the easier it is to talk about difficult
areas and share tips, the more effectively children are likely
to be parented and educated.

Most schools have rules. Many homes appear to have
none, or such informal ones that they can be interpreted i
many ways.

A good starting point with parents is to ask them some
questions, possibly as part of a parent workshop:

- What behaviour do you like in your child?

- What would you like to change or improve?

- Do you have any rules in your home? If so,
  what are they?

- When your child misbehaves, what do you
  do to alter their behaviour?

Application

Share these five simple tips for dealing with poor behaviour at a parent workshop. Explain them and then ask parents to comment on each in turn. They may already use them or have views about them that they are prepared to share.

Catch your child being successful

Praise children when they do something well that they normally find difficult: 'Well done for staying calm.' 'I liked the way you waited so patiently for us to finish eating.'

Talk things through

Find ways of rehearsing situations with children before they actually happen. This way your child is more likely to behave appropriately.

Be firm, reasonable and calm

Work out what your boundaries are and stick to them. 'Please turn the TV off now' is followed by one more firm request before you turn the TV off! Sometimes it is helpful to take a minute 'out' to calm down.

Provide a diversion

Sometimes it is better to move into another room, change the subject or use a more playful tone rather than use a sanction.

Let children experience the consequence of their behaviour

If your discipline is going to work then you need to have sanctions that you use occasionally. The clearer you are the better. And always try to be consistent.

Technique

Help with literacy

Despite successive campaigns and initiatives to improve literacy, many adults still do not feel very confident about this area. Indeed, rather than literacy, they may think of it as reading and writing. Debates about how to teach reading and apparent disagreements within the teaching profession have not helped.

There are two things that you can do to help. Be clear:

1. what you want parents to do to support you;
2. what parents might have time to do that you do not

In the first category, the most powerful thing you can do i to encourage parents to read to and with their children. Getting parents to show an interest in books and reading must be every teacher's hope.

In the second category, you could produce lists of good books, recommend good websites and encourage all parents to join a local library. You could create lists of enjoyable word games, both simple and 'bought'. You might like to create a 'bank' of story sacks (see opposite) for parents to take home. You can create lots of story sack and then you can encourage parents to do the same.

Application

A story sack is a large cloth bag containing a storybook and lots of supporting materials, such as puppets, soft toys, maps, pictures, tapes/CDs, games and so on. They are a great way to help parents get children enthused about books.

1. Choose your story, making sure that you think about the age and gender of the child who might use it.

2. Get a sack and decorate it in some way (an old cut-down pillow case will do).

3. Fill it with stimulating objects like:

   - a CD, cassette or video of the story;
   - things to make puppets, games, props and costumes;
   - a non-fiction book to learn more about situations or items in the story;
   - photos of related places or events;
   - maps relevant to the story;
   - a game or toy that is related to the story;
   - relevant artefacts;
   - related colouring books.

Technique

Help with numeracy

For some parents, modern maths is so different from what they learned at school that they are fearful of trying to help in any way. As a precaution, you could lay on some demonstration lessons to show how you do the basics of adding, subtracting, dividing and multiplying in your school. Each year, focus on a new topic like shapes or formulae, for example.

As with literacy, the key thing is for you to explain what is the minimum you expect and hope for, and then to provide lots of other ideas for parents to pick up on.

The most important thing you can encourage parents to do is to have fun with maths, finding everyday opportunities to do it with their family. This includes playing games (like chess, backgammon, cribbage, darts, dominoes and 'Battleships'), going shopping, telling the time, studying football/rugby league tables, planning holidays and many other common activities.

TIP:
Create a list of all the mathematical things that you would like parents to do at home, and regularly send home suggestions from it for people to try.

Application

Hold a taster morning or evening at school where parents can experience a range of everyday numeracy activities, which they can then try at home. Below are five examples, but you can think of many more.

■ **Games** – snakes and ladders, cribbage, darts, dominoes and other games that depend on numbers, counting, calculation and scoring.

■ **Hobbies** – comparisons of relative engine sizes, fuel economy, speed and performance or cars. Lists of statistics such as the number of weeks each single is in the charts. Sports that involve scoring, timing, counting and measuring.

■ **Patterns and shapes** – look at these on floors, wallpaper, plants, animals, and buildings. Draw or photograph objects made entirely of triangles, rectangles or squares. Make coat hanger mobiles that balance.

■ **Time** – use clocks. Estimate how long activities will take. Work out how long it is until the next mealtime. Think about calendars and dates. Make a timeline that includes the birthdays of each member of a family. Use months, weeks and days, even hours, minutes and seconds.

■ **Cooking** – have lots of recipe examples and enjoy measuring and estimating.

Technique

School transitions

It is an astonishing and worrying fact that, when many pupils move from primary to secondary school, their attainment and confidence levels go down not up. And any parent will know the stress for their children (and for them) of choosing a first nursery or primary school.

Many schools already do excellent work in familiarizing children with their new environment, and minimizing the inevitable challenges that a significant change like this brings. So what more can schools do? The answer is deceptively simple. They can really invest time and energy in supporting parents as they help their children through any transition.

At these transition periods, parents are determined to do the best for their child and yet often feel overwhelmed by unfamiliar data. One useful response by schools is to give all new parents a pack suggesting lots of things that they can do to help make the transition a positive experience for their children. As well as a warm letter of welcome and the normal useful information about your school, you could include some of the information suggested on p16 and p22, and a list of practical suggestions.

Application

Your list of ideas for parents to try might include:

- Expect the transition to be successful and be positive about it.

- Well before it's time for a transition, get into the habit of encouraging your child to try new things.

- Visit the new school as many times as possible.

- Attend all events laid on by the school to welcome new parents and children.

- Plan and rehearse the journey to school, ideally walking it.

- Meet children who went to the school last year and who have settled in happily.

- Talk about feelings, stressing how natural it is for children to feel apprehensive.

- Where children have concerns, talk through two or three practical things they could do to overcome them.

- Plan and buy all the new school equipment together.

- If you normally work, take the first few mornings of a new term off so that you can support your child.

- For children going to secondary schools, openly discuss the choice of schools.

There are many other things that your school could do and which you can add in. Some – like meeting pupils from last year's intake – have practical implications.

Gateways to specialist services

Many parents have very little idea of what they can do if they think their child needs specialist help. Who provides teachers in your school with additional specialist advice? What other local support services are there? Is every member of the teaching staff able to answer these questions? If not, then it is unlikely that parents will be!

In the UK, all schools need to be aware of The Code of Practice on the Identification and Assessment of Special Educational Needs, which came into effect in 1994. The 1996 Education Act also made it clear that schools must consider what the Code of Practice says when they draw up policies for children with special educational needs.

Parents must be told:

- the name of the teacher who is responsible for children with special educational needs, often called the Special Educational Needs Co-ordinator, or SENCO for short;

- the school's arrangements for deciding which children need special help and their plans for giving that help, stage by stage;

- how the school plans to work closely with the parents.

(From The Education Act 1996)

Application

Create a flow chart for all parents to show exactly how you manage your role as the 'gateway' to specialist services.

Use these ideas to develop your own:

1. Talk to the class teacher/form tutor.

2. Talk to the teacher responsible for special educational needs in the school.

3. If necessary, the school, with the help of outside experts, will consider the information collected so far on your child's special educational needs and the action already taken, and think about what further help your child needs.

4. Your child's teachers and the outside specialist will then draw up a new individual education plan. The school will keep a close check on how your child is doing and will record the progress carefully. You will be kept informed and invited to review meetings.

5. The outcome of a review may be that your child does not seem to be making as much progress as expected. The headteacher will decide whether to ask the local education authority to consider your child for statutory assessment, which may lead to a Statement.

6. Only a very small number of children (some two in 100) have severe and complex educational needs that require additional resources or alternative provision.

Developing roles for parents

5

Technique

Occasional help

What do you expect of your parents? How do you currently involve them in school activities? Does your school have a very small core of active parents who are prepared to help out? If so, have you asked the other parents why they do not or cannot help?

Most schools would like to have more occasional help, whether it is parents sharing their hobbies or skills informally at primary level or, for example, working as paid school-examination invigilators. Of course, it's an interesting question as to whether schools should need parent volunteers rather than professional staff! But most educators agree that involving parents is a way of enriching the lives of pupils beyond the core education that they can offer.

Many parents simply do not know what is involved, and fear that it would be too time consuming. Some simply never learn how to become involved in ways that suit their lifestyle.

Two things may help. Catch them early. Establish the habit of parental involvement when their children start at primary or secondary school. And produce a clear menu of possible volunteering options, with the amount of time and your expectations against each type of help.

The PTA is only one of the roles that parents can play and, for many, it is not an attractive one. Think more creatively about the different ways in which you can harness the skills and energies of your parents for the benefit of all your pupils.

Application

Keep an up-to-date register of parents' skills and availability by asking all parents a few simple questions. This could be done by a paper questionnaire. It could be a good excuse to speak to a parent on the telephone. You could even do it online! Explain that you are keen to find out more about the many talents that exist among parents with a view to encouraging them to share a little time with children.

Use these questions to stimulate your own:

- Do you play or coach any sport? If so, what?

- Do you have any hobbies that might interest children?

- Do you like reading to children?

- Do you have a job that children might like to find out more about?

- Do you have a few hours a month you could spend helping at school?

- What times of the day work best for you?

- What could we do to make it easier for you to give occasional time to help children at school?

Technique

Lunchtimes

One good way to engage parents is to recruit them as paid lunchtime supervisors. As well as their obvious supervision duties, you may be able to encourage them to take on a broader role beyond their core hours. This could include:

- helping to create a community kitchen;
- teaching children traditional playground games;
- reading to children;
- making music with children;
- gardening with children;
- promoting parental involvement in your school.

It may be that you can encourage parents to provide voluntary help with lunchtime clubs, or even run them. Obviously they will need to go through a security checking process, but this should not deter any who are serious about this kind of activity.

You might even inveigle some dads to run sports or computer activities at this time of day, especially if you set them up as short-term taster clubs in the first instance.

Application

 most schools find that parents who get involved often do
so circuitously. They come to school with one thing in
mind and end up doing something else. So why not make
a virtue of this and assume that if you create some kind of
social or personal learning opportunity for parents, they
may well move on to become involved in other things?

School trips

Would you like to be able to write a letter like this every term?

I would like to start this letter with a huge thank you to all the parents who have helped with a great variety of activities over the past few weeks. I know that groups of you have been to the cathedral, to Music Festival rehearsals, on the geography field trip, helping with many away fixtures, planting our wildlife area and involved in scientific investigations of every kind during Science Week. All these activities enrich the curriculum the school provides, and we simply would not be able to carry them out without your support. Many thanks!

Or maybe you already can?

It is odd that, while the legal concept governing schools is 'in loco parentis' (in place of the parent) there is still resistance by some teachers to involving parents on trips. There are two possible reasons for this. The first is to do with mind-set, the sense that teachers alone have the necessary skills. The second is more to do with the necessary organization that involving parents takes.

You might at least like to address the second of these!

etting up a database of parent volunteers will help you
with school trips and other activities.

1. Mount a campaign to persuade parents that volunteering is
   worthwhile and benefits children's education, using parent-
   volunteer advocates to help you.

2. Run a social evening with food and drink to tell parents
   more about the range of volunteering opportunities. Provide
   information about the things that parents might have to do
   on a trip.

3. Create a database showing skills, time available and the
   kinds of volunteering that each parent might consider.

4. Organize criminal record checks (www.crb.gov.uk) on all
   those who are likely to be working directly with children,
   bearing in mind that this process typically takes about four
   weeks.

5. Send regular, simple information bulletins, ideally using
   emails.

6. Enjoy the extra parent help!

Technique

Parent representatives and councils

Ever heard of a parent rep? Or of a parent council? In several countries, many schools have parent representatives who collectively form a parent council. (Think of tutor group reps sitting on a student council of some kind to give you an idea of what this might be like.)

At the simplest level, parent reps are living proof that the school wants a deeper level of engagement with parents than a PTA and occasional parent/teacher meetings can provide. The parent rep acts as a voice for common educational concerns (like the build-up to exams) or school issues. He or she can also provide a useful focus for discussions about the particular developmental needs of children in each year of school. Parent reps promote mutual understanding (between the teacher and parents) and act as conduits for a two-way flow of information. Sometimes a parent rep might suggest that a whole class/parent meeting on a topic of common interest could be arranged.

Each class or tutor group might typically nominate a parent rep. Parent reps can also form a parent council, which might meet once or twice a term with members of school staff and governors. Alternatively, you could hold parent forums once or twice a term to give parents a regular opportunity to discuss school issues of concern to them.

Application

If you are thinking about setting up a parent council or forum, then there are three key stages:

1. Thinking about what its role might be.

2 Selecting parent reps and planning a first meeting.

3. Revising the role of the group in the light of the views of its members.

In the UK, a recent research project carried out by the DfES and Human Scale Education (Human Scale Education: Setting Up Parents' Councils Project 2004–05) found these issues to be important:

■ Getting the support of the headteacher.

■ Being clear about roles and responsibilities from the outset.

■ Consulting parents from the start.

■ Not moving too fast.

■ Having some early wins so that parents really see that their voice counts.

■ Supporting parents.

■ Making time.

■ Holding meetings at parent-friendly times.

■ Creating a meeting environment that is relaxed as well as purposeful.

■ Having meetings with short, achievable agendas.

Parents as mentors

Parent-mentor schemes are common in the USA and learning mentors are increasingly becoming part of the British educational landscape.

A parent mentor is someone who has some skills and experiences to offer to young people. Already a parent (and therefore likely to understand children), parent mentors might, for example, focus on working with:

- disadvantaged pupils
- talented pupils
- 'difficult' pupils
- 'coasting' pupils.

Mentors might also focus on helping pupils from particular cultural backgrounds to learn and acquire more self-confidence.

Sometimes mentors are drawn from a deliberately similar cultural or social background to their potential mentees, but sometimes the reverse is true. Typically a mentor would arrange to see a pupil for a series of 20, 30 or 40-minute one-to-one sessions lasting perhaps half a term.

Application

ou might like to work your way through these ten steps
 set up a parent-mentor scheme:

1. Work out what you are trying to achieve.

2. Decide which pupils you are trying to mentor.

3. Recruit potential mentors, both from parents and other sources.

4. Prepare your mentors.

5. Prepare the pupils as to what to expect.

6. Work out some simple success measures (for example, numbers of mentors, pupil attendance and so on).

7. Make sure you allocate one member of staff to co-ordinate the programme.

8. Arrange for mentors to have ongoing feedback.

9. Run security checks.

10. Get started.

dapted from a leaflet published by the Mentoring and
friending Foundation, www.mandbf.org.uk)

Technique

Teaching Assistants

How many of your teaching assistants are also parents?

Many schools have found that parents are the natural plac
to start when it comes to recruiting teaching assistants
(TAs). And doubtless the TAs you have are involved in all
the normal in-service and professional training that other
members of staff are.

But what about a less formal and voluntary kind of
teaching assistant? The simplest way to see if there is
interest among parents is to write to them. Given many
people's busy lives, you are unlikely to be deluged! But
assuming that you get at least one potential volunteer,
then (once you have been through the security checks)
you can begin.

You might like to:

- invite them to informally observe you;

- talk to other colleagues who already use parent
  helpers;

- get them to follow a particular pupil for an hour;

- provide them with some simple 'how to' informatior
  about what they might do;

- get them started;

- make sure you connect with them each time they
  help so that they feel valued;

- say a few words of thanks and get their feedback
  before they leave.

Application

Parent volunteers can be used in a wide variety of ways.
Choose ideas from here that you like – and add your own!

cutting, tracing, collating

reading with small groups

reading with individuals

working with a child on a special project

one-to-one work on literacy

one-to-one work on numeracy

helping with homework

photography

publishing pupil books

music

artwork

working in school grounds

Technique

PTA

Most schools have a PTA or parent/teacher association. And when you say the letters PTA, most teachers have very distinct reactions; they either welcome parents' practical contributions to school life or dread the well-intentioned interference!

PTAs are open, as their name suggests, to parents and teachers, as well as others in the school community. Their aim is to foster better relationships between parents and their children's schools, and to create a partnership that helps the school to listen to and deal with parents' concerns. They allow parents to learn more about what they can do to help the school, and can provide an excellent forum for communication and a base for partnership between parents and school.

PTAs do many different things including:

- fundraising
- organizing events
- organizing catering
- helping develop school grounds
- promoting better understanding of education and school issues
- providing an informal forum for discussion.

Application

>w well is your PTA doing? Use these questions to
ompt some thinking. You might like to use them to hold
reflective discussion with your current PTA members.

- How many people regularly come to PTA meetings?

- How many people regularly give up time to help at PTA
  events?

- What did your PTA do last year?

- What does your PTA plan to do this year?

- How much money did the PTA raise last year?

- What were the best things that your PTA did last year?

- How highly is your PTA thought of?

- What would you like your PTA to do that it is not doing
  now?

Technique

Parent governors

Parent governors are important members of any school's governing body. They are elected by other parents at the school to serve for four years. They must be a parent of a child on the school roll at the time of their election. If their child leaves the school before the end of their term of office, they may continue to the end of their term of office.

Although elected by parents, parent governors do not have to represent any views apart from their own. They may, however, wish to express other parents' views to the governing body where appropriate.

Parent governors tend to receive any complaints about the school from parents, as they may be seen as closer to parents. But parent governors are full governors, take part in all aspects of the work of the governing body and have to take their collective governance responsibilities just as seriously as any other governor.

Being a parent governor is an onerous and worthwhile role that few parents will necessarily want to undertake. The advantage of having a range of strategies for involving parents in the life of your school is that you are much more likely to attract high-calibre candidates for the parent-governor role.

Application

ou might like to try some of these ideas to recruit and tain parent governors:

- Use existing parent governors to help 'recruit' their successors.

- Get potential parent governors involved in other aspects of helping the school first.

- Create a jargon-free description of the role.

- If there is an election, encourage candidates to be creative in the way they produce biographies about themselves.

- Pair all new parent governors with a mentor who can help them through the early stages.

- Pay parent governors to attend training sessions.

- Make sure you spend time with your parent governor.

- Make sure you use the skills and time of a parent governor well by explicitly asking what he or she would like to do once settled in.

Technique

Parents as lifelong learners

Of course, one of the most interesting ways in which you could decide to engage parents is by offering them a chance to carry on learning for themselves, rather than in their role as a parent. Many community secondary schools already run a thriving programme of formal classes in the twilight hours. Some also lay on more informal activities, related, for example, to sports, arts or leisure facilities that they possess.

It is all too easy to forget that most schools are not used after 6pm in the evening and at weekends. However, with a bit of imagination it is possible to create all kinds of opportunities for parents, their friends and members of the local community.

Sometimes it will be possible to fund these from external sources. Your school might benefit from offering space to local groups, especially if you are able to provide somewhere for parents with specific common interests, or from a particular cultural group.

Stop and review the way you are using your site. Remember: most parents become volunteers because they start doing something at your school and begin to see it and you in a new light!

Application

Think of some groups who might like to run sessions at your school:

- Local colleges
- Tennis clubs
- Keep-fit clubs
- Youth groups
- Faith groups.

Think of some new services your school could offer parents and local people, their friends and members of the community:

- Photocopying facilities
- Printing services
- Summer classes
- Sports facilities
- Media studies equipment.

You can think of many more!

> I've just found out that there's something called lifelong learning after you leave school!

Reaching parents who are turned off from school

Technique

How people get turned off from learning

Cultural	• Suspicion of clever people
	• Lack of previous opportunity in the family
	• For some women, a feeling that it is a man's world
	• For some men, a feeling that learning is not for real men
	• A tradition of leaving school and going straight into a job
	• Alienation through high unemployment
	• Peer pressure
Structural	• Lack of money
	• Lack of time
	• Lack of childcare
	• Disability
	• Lack of information, advice and guidance
Personal	• Unhappy school memories
	• Language issues
	• Low motivation
	• Low self-esteem
	• Health
	• Age
	• Learning styles not seeming compatible with what is on offer

Chances are that many of the parents you really want to meet and engage have themselves become switched off from learning.

Sadly, many people think of school as a place where they first learnt tough lessons about failure and rejection. As parents, these people may be suspicious about schools and teachers. There can also be cultural barriers to becoming involved. See if these ideas can help you to reach out to those who are turned off from school.

Application

learning is fun!

Learning pays!

Using the chart on the opposite page, come up with as many different ways of addressing these barriers to learning as possible. For example:

Unhappy school memories

Create a short film of children enjoying a range of activities at your school, with clips of parents talking about how much they feel involved.

Age

Invite local senior citizens to come and have lunch in the school canteen and take part in an activity once a month, so that children and parents see that you are never too old to start learning.

Technique

Second languages

The most obvious way in which parents can feel excluded from any school is if they simply do not speak your language. Deeper cultural issues can also widen this barrier.

If your school has a significant number of parents (and/or children) whose first language is not English, then you are probably already skilled in outreach work and may have specialist home/school liaison staff working with you. Special effort will often be required to engage with parents, especially mothers, and in some cases they may find home visits, or meetings on 'neutral territory', easier than coming to school.

Some schools deliberately set up cultural events related to the different cultures present in the school, for example to coincide with Eid or Diwali.

How you choose to approach this issue depends on your mind-set. If you see the fact that only a proportion of parents speak English as a barrier, then you may be cutting off a valuable source of education and development. Cultural diversity can provide an enormous educational opportunity for all children at your school, and you may want to invest considerable effort in developing opportunities for parents whose first language is not English.

Application

o you know which languages parents speak? Do you
now where they come from? Do you know which
eligions are represented and what the major festivals are?
o you know about any cultural taboos that there may be
mong certain groups? Do you know if there are any
upplementary or mother-tongue schools in your area?

nowledge is educational power and you might like to
make sure that you have and use this kind of basic but
mportant knowledge. For each language you could
ompile a table like this:

Language:	
Number of speakers	
Religion(s)	
Key festivals	
Taboos	
Actions planned by the school	

Technique

Family learning outreach activities

On p40 we explored the idea that you might open your school to families of your pupils on a particular day. But what about thinking more broadly about other activities you might promote?

Throughout the year there are many 'weeks' promoting different educational activities, which you could arrange your activities to coincide with. For example, in the UK, National Science Week is in March and National Parents' Week is in October.

Two other obvious places to start would be at the weekend and during holidays. You could test the water by hosting arts, science, sports or outdoor activities occasionally at the weekend.

You could lay on a holiday play scheme and encourage your own pupils and their parents to be involved. A holiday play scheme could be a one-off experiment just for a week or you could be more ambitious and see them as a continuation of your breakfast and after-school clubs during term-time.

The BBC website www.bbc.co.uk/schools/revisewise/parents/familylearning provides a range of excellent resources for parents to use at any time.

Application

Family Learning Week is a national awareness campaign created to highlight the importance of family learning. This annual festival of learning happens every year in the UK in October and is organized by the Campaign for Learning (www.campaign-for-learning.org.uk).

Organizations throughout the country get together to put on fun activities, which are aimed at involving the whole family, from mums and dads to aunts, uncles and grandparents, as well as children.

A wide range of organizations is involved, including libraries, museums and galleries, nurseries, schools, colleges, universities, town and retail centres, sport and leisure centres, parks, zoos, heritage sites and many community and voluntary organizations.

Why not lay on a programme of activities yourself? Look at this imaginary week and adapt it to suit your school.

Monday	Joint event with local museum – exhibition of 1960s memorabilia
Tuesday	Outdoor science day with members of the local college and local farmer
Wednesday	Fairtrade day including cooking and eating a community tea
Thursday	Visit to local National Trust property in Victorian costume
Friday	Family day at school
Saturday	Orienteering fun afternoon at school

Technique

Extending schooling

Often, especially in some less affluent urban areas, a school is likely to have the best computer facilities in the area. A school's sports and catering facilities may also be better than anything available locally. Secondary schools, especially community schools, have increasingly begun to see how they can provide many more services than just teaching children.

The 'extended school' movement is trying to do just this kind of thing. An extended school is one that works with local providers (and in many cases other schools) to provide extended services, often beyond the school day, such as:

- childcare 8am–6pm, all year round;

- parenting and family support;

- activities including study support, sport and music clubs;

- community use of facilities;

- swift and easy referral to specialist services such as speech therapy and health drop-ins (see pp66–67).

If you are interested you might like to talk to the extended-schools remodelling advisor in your local authority as a first step.

Application

s part of the extended school idea, you might like to
onsider ways in which your school could act much more
s a one-stop shop for a range of services for people in
our community. This could include specialist support
ervices such as speech and language therapy, family
upport services and behaviour support, all of which could
e based at or near your school.

fact, just as some doctor's surgeries have expanded to
clude nurses, physiotherapy, homeopathy, dental
ractices and dispensing chemists, so schools could rethink
eir traditional role. They could provide access to other
cial services, banking via a cash machine, a community
st office, a community library and so on.

ften we are only bounded by our experience when it
mes to thinking what might be. Why not take a moment
dream some dreams about your schools in ten years'
ne (or sooner!)?

Technique

The school of the future

Think about a time ten years from now. What could your school provide that it does not do now?

- In what ways will it be involving parents?
- Will there be classrooms?
- Will there be a school day?
- Will holidays follow the same pattern as they do now?
- Will they look different?
- Who else will be using them?

Be as radical as you can!

Application

My future school could have...

No school subjects !

Parent forums
- help to run schools
- advise
- be imformed

a Post Office

a Doctor's surgery

maybe a Business Centre

No year groups
→ pupils move up when ready

Parents help day
Employees day

Employers release parents to help in schools

Curriculum tailored to needs of children

Further reading

Bayley, R. and Broadbent, L. (2005) *Flying Start with Literacy,* Network Educational Press

Carrington, D. and Whitten, H. (2005) *Future Directions: Practical ways to develop emotional intelligence and confidence in young people*, Network Educational Press

Teare, B. (2004) *Parents' and Carers' Guide for Able and Talented Children,* Network Educational Press

Burrell, A. and Riley, J. (eds.) (2005) *Promoting Children's Well-Being in the Primary Years,* Network Educational Press

Lucas, B. (2006) *Boost Your Mind Power Week by Week,* Duncan Baird

Lucas, B. (2006) *Happy Families: how to make one, how to keep one,* BBC Active

Lucas, B. (2005) *Discover Your Hidden Talents: the essential guide to lifelong learning,* Network Educational Press

Lucas, B. and Claxton, G. (2004) *Be Creative: essential step for life and work,* BBC Active

Lucas, B. and Smith, A. (2003) *Help Your Child to Succeed Toolkit,* Network Educational Press

Lucas, B. and Smith, A. (2002) *Help Your Child to Succeed,* Network Educational Press

Lucas, B. (2001) *Power Up Your Mind: learn faster, work smarter,* Nicholas Brealey

You may find these websites helpful:

www.alite.co.uk
www.bill-lucas.com
www.campaign-for-learning.org.uk
www.continyou.org.uk
www.education-world.com
www.hse.org.uk
www.mandbf.org.uk
www.nrich.maths.org.uk
www.parentlink.co.uk
www.parentscentre.gov.uk
www.parents.org.uk
www.standards.dfes.gov.uk/parentalinvolvement